Written by
Lindi Masters©

Illustrated by
Lizzie Masters©

Lindi Masters

Lizzie Masters

THE CUBE AND THE TWELVE STRANDS

This Book Belongs to:

_____

SeraphCreative
Heaven's Heart for Earth

A plumbline is like a cord or a strand.

They connect us from one thing to another.

In the bible we have twelve plumblines or cords that help us to walk in truth.

We know that Yeshua said He is the way and He is the truth.

All these cords are found in the Bible.

Scan the QR code to listen to the meditation on The 12 Strands.

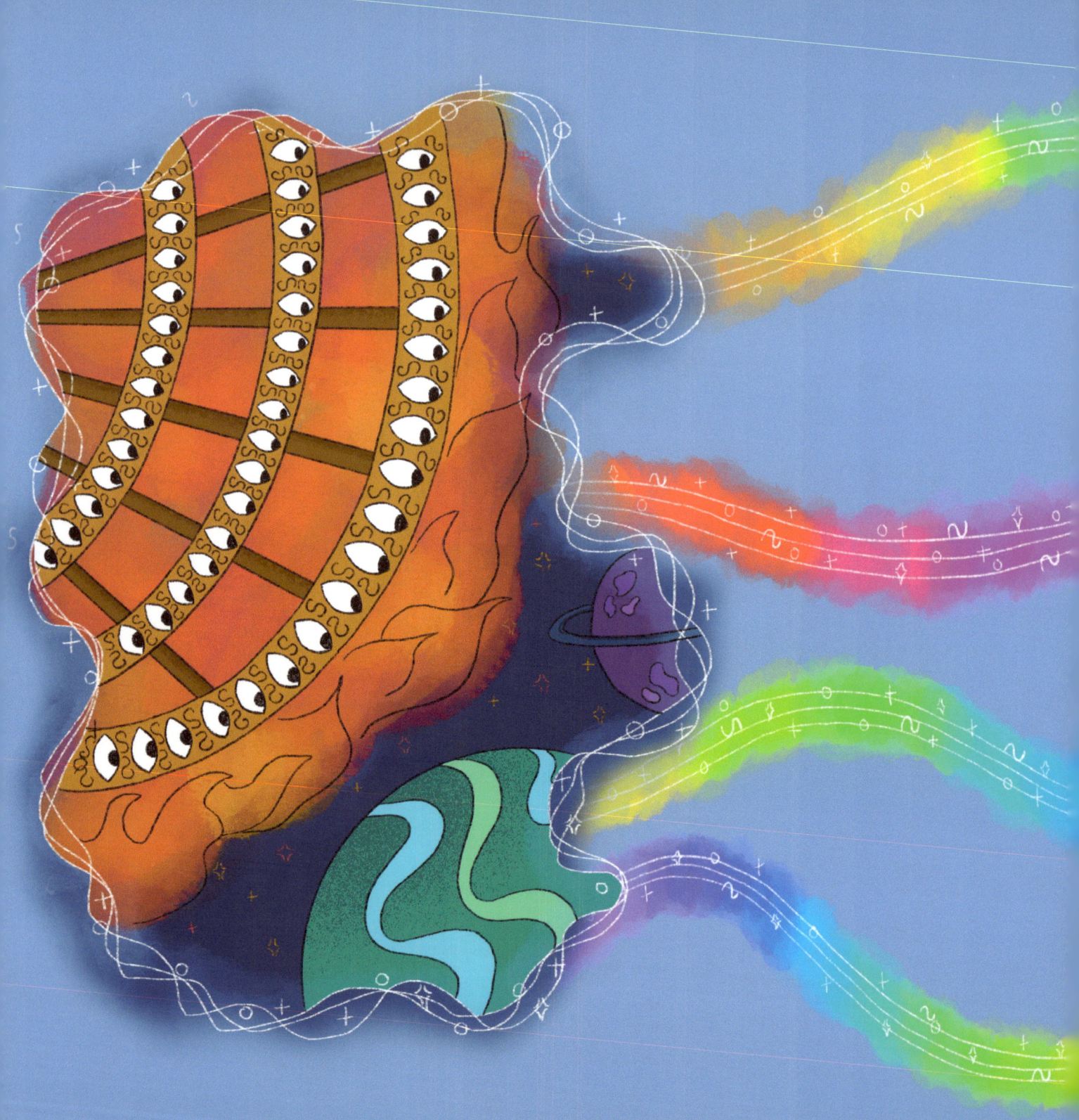

Whenever we see angels or see things in Heaven, we can use these twelve plumblines to make sure what we see is truth and is real.

The first three cords are from the Father.
They are Justice, Judgement and Mercy
(Holiness). We can find them in the Bible,
Psalm 89:14

The next three are from Yeshua. They are The Way, The Truth and The Life. This is found in John 14:6.

We can find three from the Holy Spirit, Ruach haKodesh. These are Righteousness, Peace and Joy in Romans 14:17.

The last three are the cords or plumblines that I am as a Son of Yahweh. I live, and Move, and Have My Being. This is found in Acts 17:28.

You are like a living stone being built into a spiritual house. Houses are built out of bricks that look like cubes.

Scan the QR code to listen to the meditation on The Cube.

It is like geometry in Mathematics. We call it sacred geometry. Sacred means Holy.

Inside of each of us is a spiritual cube.
1 Peter 2:4

HI!

Let's have a look at some of the cubes that sit in our hearts.

We engage with the four faces of Yahweh and as we do it brings us into being a mature Son.

Here is another cube that sits in our hearts. One of the plumblines. It is the cube of love.

Another cube is YHVH. It brings us into the Priesthood of Yahweh.

Did you know that the Cross of Yeshua can be made into a cube?

Folding Cube Tutorial

Scan and print the craft found on the next page.

Decorate and colour in your craft however you want!

Cut it out and punch through the holes.

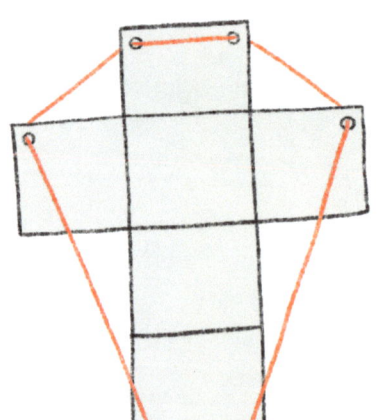

Thread string through the holes the same way it's done in the photo. Pull on the 2 string at the end to fold your cube.

Printed out Craft
Decorating Stationery
Scissors
Thread or String

YES
HUA

Twelve Strands Tutorial

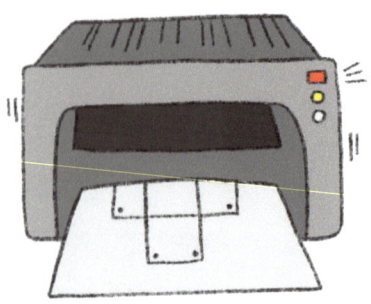

Scan and print the craft found on the next page.

Decorate and colour in your craft however you want!

Cut it out!

Stack the triangles on top of each other. Use a paper fastener or split pin in the middle of the triangles to hold them together. This will also make them able to move around.

You will need:
Printed out Craft
Decorating Stationery
Scissors
Paper fastener/Split pin

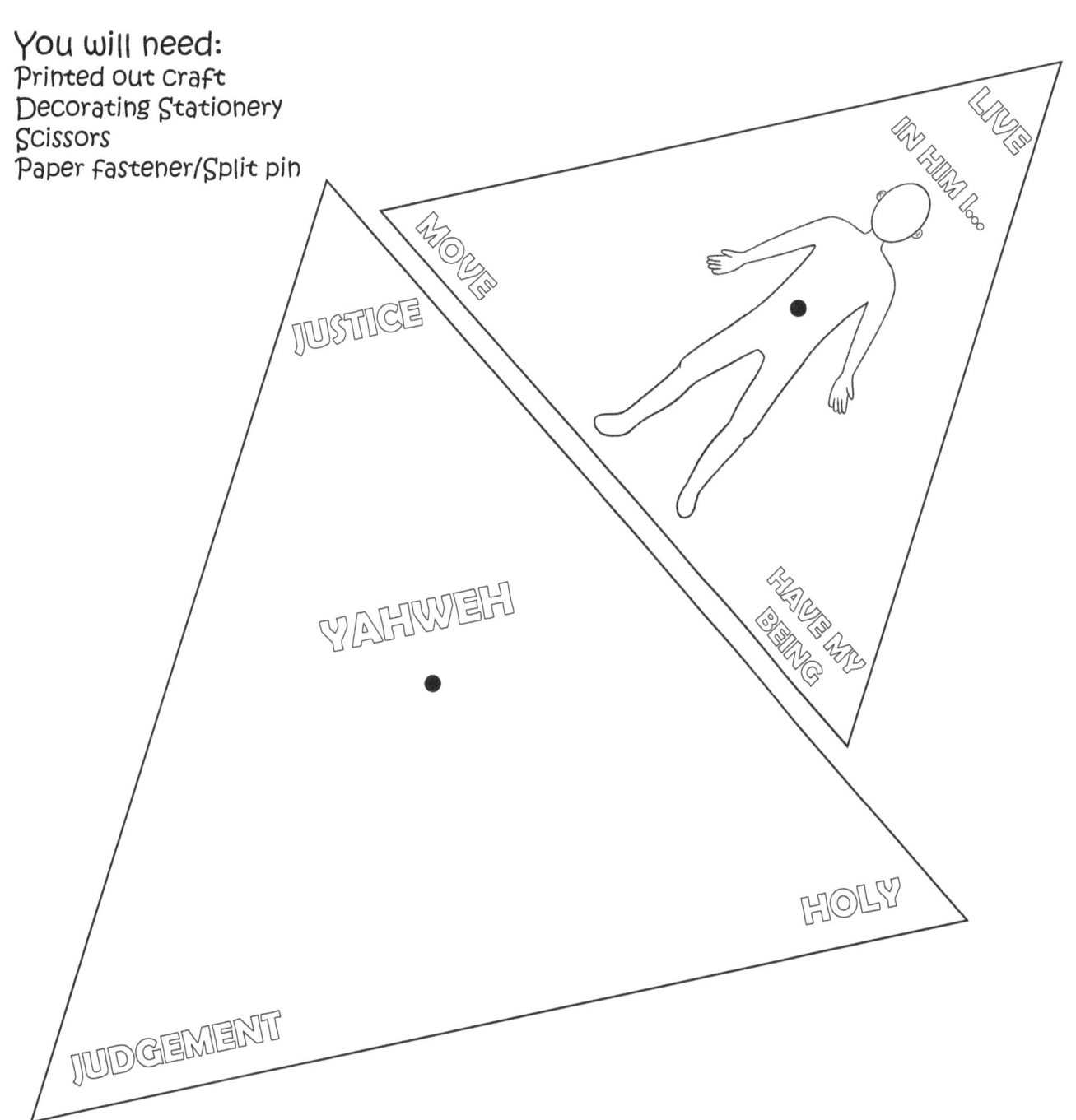

LIVE
IN HIM I...
MOVE
JUSTICE
HAVE MY
BEING
YAHWEH
HOLY
JUDGEMENT

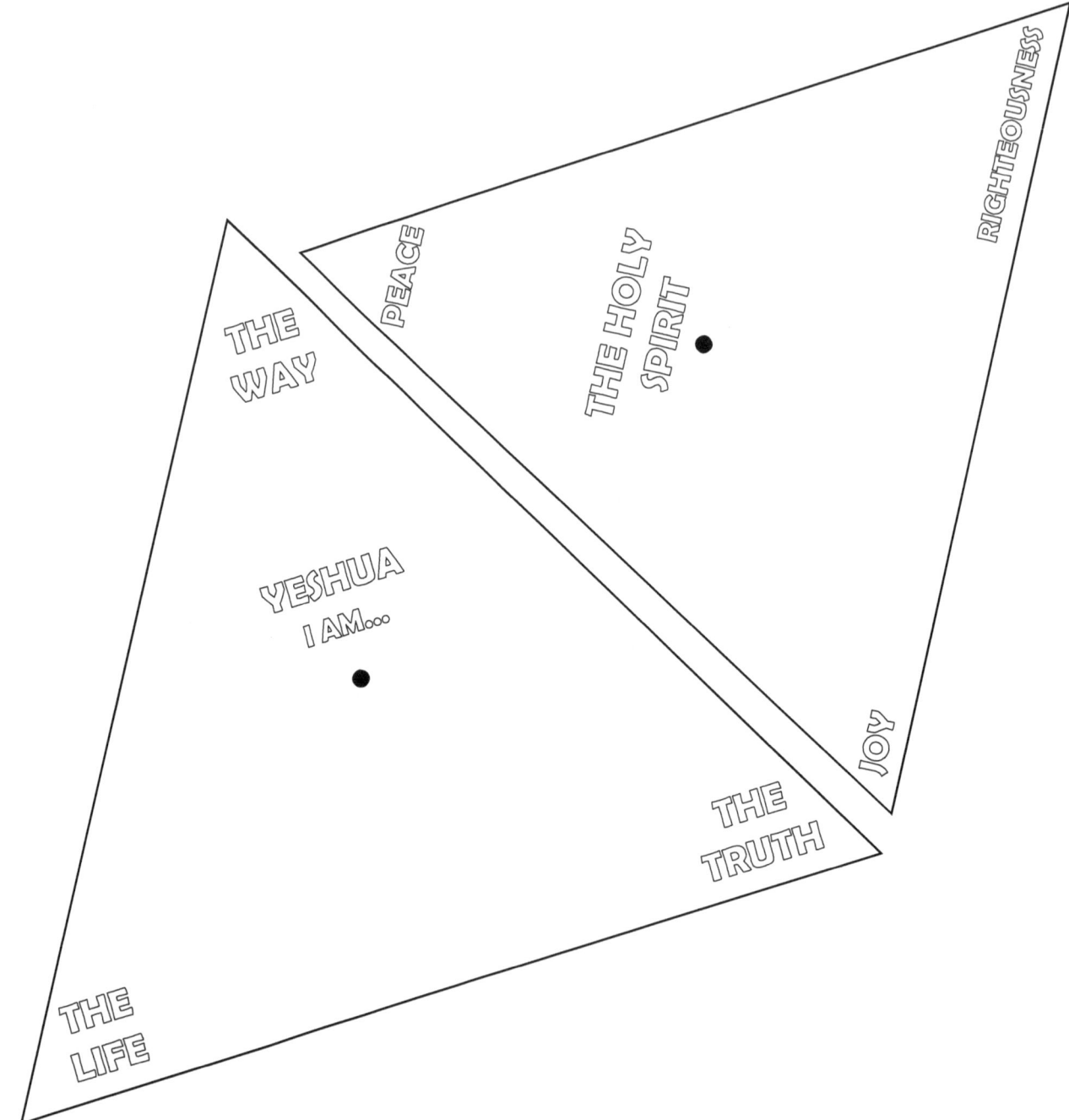

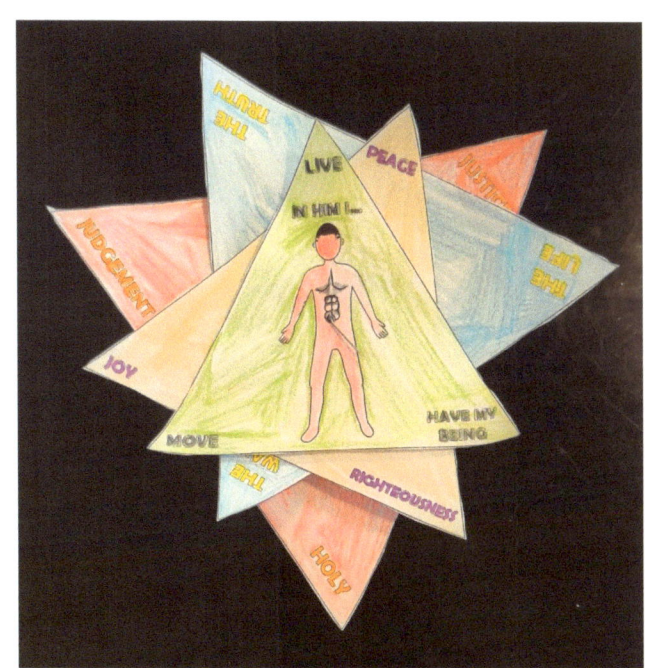